I0453935

Orphan Poetry

Alexis Cremeans

Copyright © 2025 by **The Henlo Press**

All rights reserved. This book or any portion thereof may not be reproduced or used in any manner whatsoever without the express written permission of the publisher except for the use of brief quotations in a book review.

Printed in the United States of America

First Printing, 2025

ISBN-978-1-962019-20-0

www.thehenlopress.com

The Henlo Press
P.O. Box 1694
Ashland, KY 41105

To my mother and grandmother,
The memory of you inspires me to be the best I can be. I
wish you could see what I've written for you.

To my husband,
You are what I look forward to every single day. I love you
more than words can express.

To my daughter,
In you, there is a whole world waiting to be discovered. I
hope you always know that you are everything to me.

Table of Contents

This One

For My Husband

When I think about you, everything is music.
My heartstrings play your kind of melody
and your heart beats along to my
out-of-time two-step.
Your breath constitutes the song in my head, replaying
all-day
until I let myself complete the refrain—
"I love you."

My heart sings a love song for you each morning
in words I have, as yet, never found.
As the sun lazily overcomes the horizon,
your hand crests my waist and
we greet the day together.

I am not good at love poems—
a good poem has pain mixed in,
like a country song
or a good story.
They say love hurts,
but I believe there should be
no hurt in loving.
Maybe that's why all the love songs feel hollow.
Maybe that's why I haven't written you a good love poem—
there has been no pain in loving you.

Now when we talk about this book
and you ask me,
"Is there one in there for me?"
I will think about the music in my mind
that sounds like your name–
the song my heart sings
to the time of yours beating.

All the sweet words known to me
could never express the beauty of that melody.
So I am reduced to what I have,
all of it laid bare here,
in this one.

My Dogs Saw God Today

My dogs saw God today.
The morning sun crested the horizon
like His sleepy eyes opening slowly to greet the day
and all three barked
and hawed
and could not look away,
much like myself
who barked
and hawed
and could not look away.
Though unlike them—
they stare in awe
but unknowing, uncaring
if the brightness will blind them—
Unlike them
I flinch.

Event Horizon

Sweaty, smokey summer,
      Grass green, fragrant, mower humming...
How does this picture always become a poem?

    You were not even young then,
        You have always seemed ageless and ancient
        All at once.

Now, perhaps, more so,
      Existing only as a quantum apparition.
      Are you out there,
      Somewhere in time and space?

    I have searched the farthest reaches
        Of possibility for an answer,
      Yet all I have found in the vastness
      Is myself.

    My mind is a time traveler,
        Faster than light, speeding
      Through the wormholes of my heart,
        Right to what hangs darkest
In the unending cloud of memory that is the universe
      Of my mind.

    If I could steer this mutinied heart,
        I would aim for that darkest spot,
    And upon the event horizon,

      If I were lucky,
        I would find myself,
          Frozen in time,
              In your backyard.

Like Sunlight in a Dark Place

No place exists on Earth
where the contrast of Sun and Shadow
is greater than in the forests.

Purple twilight persists throughout the day
like the will to live in the human mind.

Then, from the darkness
the blinding light of the sun breaks in,
a memory of you
from when I was happy—
when the sun didn't burn.

Here in the endless night,
it only hurts
and beckons my eyes to close.

So sudden is the onslaught of the past
that even in my escape to the shadows
the oppressive light stays with me
—a ghost behind my eyes.

Portrait of My Mother at Eighteen

I do not know what decisions
propelled her down the eventual path
of destruction,
but she could not have foreseen this
at 18.

Lost in daydreams of love?
Maybe
An adolescent quest for
Euphoria?
An escape?

I do not know if or how often
She heard her mother pray for a different life,
But I know she knew it happened.
Drummer in the high school band,
Dreaming of Kelly Green and white,
Her future could not have been sealed
As she fantasized about
A Native American love affair,
Scratched on pages of notebook paper.

Songs sung in joy in the bright sun
Of an amphitheater spotlight.
I can only imagine
How she felt
When it went out.

She is the Coming Winter

Do not compare her to a summer's day.
She is not humid, blinding, or muggy.
The air inside her is not stagnant,

rather it is mobile—
twisting and turning,
dancing through trees,
whispering of the storm and cold to come.

She is not soft like a flower in spring—
that is a different sort of fragile.
She is brittle like a dying leaf;
on the breath of the wind,
she flies away.

She hangs on for far too long,
then the setting of the summer sun beckons her.
Downward
where she will be forgotten, trodden on,
Decaying.

Do not compare her to a summer's day
but an autumn's,
for she heralds a coming winter.

And she is beautiful—
the final remnants
of the world before the cold.

Trees in California

There is too much air above me:
my bumbling tongue too big for my
meek little mouth.
I feel the oppression of the unknowable past
and looming future
as a promise waiting to break my heart.
To breathe is to shatter.
I am coursing with poison.

There are trees in California
3,000 years older than Christ—
he surely visited them on his tour
of the States.
Maybe took a branch or bark for a souvenir.
"I was here."

The Other Side of Sunset

Sudden awareness.

He walks, he knows not where, as his eyes adjust to the blinding light of the sun. His skin is soaked in sweat, bare, and exposed to the baking heat. Whatever stretch of flesh he can see on himself is red and will surely blister. But he feels no discomfort, only the wetness of perspiration.

He is not hot.
His skin does not hurt.
He is just wet.

This must mean I'm dying.

His bare feet kick up the powder-soft sand of the desert he finds himself in. This place has been filled and turned over by the wind so many times, that there is not one inch of it that has ever, or will ever, be the same. He feels the grains nestle under his toenails and in the webs of his feet, in the hairs on his legs and arms. The sweat dampening his skin clings to each piece, coating him in a fine layer of grit.

Fry me like a breaded chicken.
I must be dying.

Trudging onward, he claws desperately for a memory of how he got to this place, but all he remembers is a drink.

How long has it been since I had a drink?

He cannot remember the last time he felt this thirsty.

There are many types of thirsty.
How long has it been?
Perhaps I'll put my tongue to skin.

Like a snake eating his own tail, he licks the sweat from his lips and feels as though Christ poured for him His own wine.

There are many types of thirsty.
How long has it been?

He sat alone in a bar. He did not seek company, only somewhere to sit. Beer in hand, he stared at the countertop, dwelling on how heavy the world had become and how strained his back had grown from the weight. Standing required all the strength he could muster, and he would rather sit at that bar and let time tick by without him than to face the world another day. Forty years had already gone by with barely a blink from his eyes. How bad could forty more be if he sat here, drinking them away?

Forty years—
How long has it been?
Forty years.

The desert sun begins its descent, taking with it the heat that would be the end of him. Now he remembers the true worry in the desert—the frigid night.

Darkness keeps coming,
But so does the morning.

Can I last till morning?

The only thing to do is keep walking. This desert is unforgiving. It offers no shelter, no timber, no water. Only day, night, and the gift of unbounded direction.

This desert is as broad as the universe.
Why did I choose to walk this way?
Which way is the sun?

He acknowledges the sun setting behind him, himself walking further into darkness. The stars are blooming in front of him; behind him the sky is bruising, then blazing, igniting on the horizon as that life-bringing light says its goodbye with beauty and color.

Why did I choose to walk this way?
Darkness keeps coming.
Which way is the sun?

He contemplates the reality of his situation, his increasingly desperate need for warmth and water; yet still he is awed at the lack of sensation he feels. Not only the lack of panic or despair, or even confusion but the almost total lack of physical sensation. The night quickly creeps up on him, but he doesn't feel the chill of the darkness. He does not feel the sun on his back as it transitions to bless the other end of the world.

Darkness keeps coming,
But so does the morning.
I chose to walk this way…

The numbness is fitting, familiar. The lack of sensation reminds him of his nights spent drinking, soaking himself in liquor until his eyes could no longer see the truth right in front of him.

He was alone in the bar

Alone in a bar
How long has it been?

Forty years…
and she was home, waiting on him to call

I wonder if she'll answer when I call.

She probably answered, because she always answers. He probably yelled at her, because he always yells at her.

She always says she's had enough.

Maybe she ditched him on the highway.

Maybe hit my head first.
Gabby, honey, my head hurts.

He probably called and she probably answered. He probably yelled at her because he probably had a hard day.

I never get one easy day.

She probably said she had enough and told him to kick rocks, and he probably said,

Fine, stop the car. I'll walk.

And she probably said

Walk where?

Anywhere else

But he probably didn't say it. He probably just walked.

Only way through is forward.
Darkness keeps coming,
but so does the morning.

The night is fully on him now. The bruise of the sunset has blackened, dark purple heart deepening to an inky black as the light of day completes one cycle and begins another. Still, he feels nothing but the sand between his toes as he walks. Suddenly, light up ahead perches on the horizon.

Why did I choose this way?
Which way is the sun?

His head is spinning, aching, as the chill begins to creep into his fingers. Only slightly, but he no longer feels comfortable. This night is long, and the light up ahead is not sunlight.
Who builds a home in this wasteland?

If there's heat, it's home enough.
Darkness keeps coming.

He has been walking so long, it feels unnatural to stand still at the front door. The house…

My house, our house

is lit from within, and the door is unlocked. All this walking and he is not prepared to walk through the front door.

Who builds a home in this wasteland?
I chose this way.

His hands shake as he reaches for the door, half afraid it's an illusion, half afraid it isn't. She's probably inside, still mad, and she'll probably say,

Anywhere else, huh?

and he'll probably say nothing.

Only way through is forward.
Darkness keeps coming.
Which way is the sun?
I chose this way.

He opens it, and the house is lit but empty. There is no sound of music, TV, talking, or shouting. It is silent except for the sound of his trembling and the faint patter of the running shower.

Maybe she is home.

He calls, and there's no answer. She's probably still mad, and he's probably still drunk but he feels the need to see. He needs to see for himself.

How long has it been?
Forty years...
There are different kinds of thirsty.
Which way is the sun?

He walks quietly through this house, here in the desert, a miracle just in the making.

Mistakes are miracles in disguise.
I chose this way.
Darkness keeps coming,
But so does the morning.

He walks into the bedroom, all lights on, the shower running, water pounding like his heartbeat. He still feels the dampness of old sweat and the chill of the desert night on his skin.

Naked.
Alone in a bar.
Which way is the sun?
Why did I choose this way?

His hands find the nightstand even as his eyes glaze over, used to reaching for her phone in the cover of darkness. Does he want to look?

The only way through is forward.
Darkness keeps coming.

The screen's glow is miniscule in the full illumination of every light in the house. Still glazed, barely comprehending, his eyes dance through the light, so much light—light intense like the brightness of the desert in daytime. It scorches tears into his eyes.

Darkness keeps coming
But so does the morning.
The only way through is forward.
I chose this way.

And when he was done, betrayal revealed, the blackness of the locked screen was darker than the frigid night.

The only way through is forward
Which way is the sun?
Darkness keeps coming.
Why did I choose this way?

Through the window in the bedroom, he sees the faintest light on the horizon as the sun begins another cycle, blessing this end of the world with daylight once again. Out there, in the direction he had been walking, the heat of day is building. Within, with lights on, he feels the lingering chill of night.

Darkness keeps coming.

He steps away from the nightstand, walks through the bedroom, and into the bathroom.

I chose this way.

And she's probably still mad, and he's probably still drunk, but it's the only way he feels like he can say it.

How long has it been?
I know, now.
Forty years.
There are different kinds of thirsty.
The only way through is forward.
Who builds a home in this wasteland?

Anywhere else.

The shower curtain's sharp rattle wakes him.

"Oh my God, are you okay?"

It takes him a minute to get his bearings. He expected to see Gabby standing in the shower, anger, and heat from the water flushing her cheeks, tears collecting in her lashline but blending in with the rivulets from the showerhead above. But instead, he lay on the shower floor, cold water pelting his skin. Above him, his coworker Bill.

"You didn't call in…again, so Sharon suggested somebody come check on you. We couldn't get a hold of Gabby either, so…"

Mistaking the source of confusion, Bill adds, "My dad's a locksmith, so I volunteered. And we're buddies, so I figured you wouldn't mind…especially if you're hurt…Hey, do you need help up or do you, like, want some pants?"

He checks in with himself, with reality. Bill, the big oaf, looks sheepishly at the floor and the vanity for signs of a towel.

"Bill, I'm alright man. Or I will be, anyway. Just shut the door there, buddy, and I'll be out in a second."

Bill asks no further questions and gratefully turns his back, shutting the door gingerly behind him.

Shaky legs stand him up. Trembling hands tie a towel around his waist. Red, stinging eyes flutter back at him in the mirror. His skin is shriveled from the water, goosebumps prickling his arms and legs.

How long has it been?

He remembers the bar.

Alone in a bar.

And a fight in the car.

Fine, let me out, I'll walk.

And a cold night.

Naked, alone.
I went through her phone.

But something begins to warm him from within or perhaps from the window.

Why did I choose this way?

It seems as though the sun may just be rising.

The only way through is forward.

And just as it will set again this evening, he knows that on the other end of the darkness...

I chose this way

is, inevitably, another sunrise.

And so did the morning.

A Blue Sky

Recently, my vision has been plagued by pastel colors.

I have not seen a blue sky in ages;

my breath has not been swept away by the wind

in

    so

       long,

that it has ceased to even course through my lungs.

This weather,

        Abysmal.

This year,

        Abysmal.

I only find solace in the promise of

someday, again,

a blue sky.

It is a Mad World

Time passes unannounced and the stars tick by overhead
          like a child's carousel.
Conversation runs in 4/4 time,
and we rent words from the eternal sky.
We give the words their worth.

Our world is a spark inside a fish tank at the bottom
          of the ocean—
our view of the sun is lost through leagues of filthy water.
We crawl dumbly, blindly into the cold dark depths,
ignorant of the sky.

We think ourselves as masters of our unknown reality and search
for enlightenment
by exploring dark places—
We are creatures of irony.
We presume ourselves significant enough to dictate the past
with just a word.
We brew in arrogant primordial soup.

We are all Ocean Divers in our own minds.
Dig far enough to fall through the sky.
Question.
Everything we know is a story.
Who's telling it?
Where would we be without the omnipotent narrative?

All of our concepts revolve around greed.
Our words are monetary and cold.
Our society is cold,
reflected in a black mirror to dumb faces, agape mouths,
          and obscene intentions.

Ass u me y ou kno w th e f ace of G odd.
Ass u me no thing.

Guess and be rejected,
eternal is the mystery of the ether.
Long in vain for knowledge while you pass by Time's face
as a dust mote in a ray of sun.
Time's breath is your destruction.

Feel the intense weight of humanity in the base of your skull.
Let it pull you back on yourself.

Feel reality bend.
Feel the world end.

Reminders of God

Dusky diamonds
gracing a sinful city with their glory in a streetlight—
the streets, at night,
louder than life,
thriving.
We are thriving;
we are weeds sprouting from the cracks in the concrete of our
foundations,
crumbling.

Arrogant and in awe of ourselves,
the city is a funhouse mirror—
distorting,
distracting.
Puddles, not rain.
Ego, no brain.

We sacrificed our stars to Moloch.
Behold,
the price of industry and greed.
But our buildings will not surmount Everest.
Our legacies will be devoured by the sun.

Watch as the moon pulls the ocean's puppet strings,
bask in the life that a summer rain brings.
When our dirty clouds have parted
and we reunite with the sky,
we will walk our crumbled streets starving
for reminders of a once-forsaken god.

A Poem Hides

In the song of birds at dawn,

echoing gently through the gnarled branches

of trees worn by winter

and rain.

In the pattering of the rain

on the new tin roof,

brick red,

to hide the inevitable rust

as it ages.

In the memories of ages past,

ghostly like the brooding morning,

veiled by mist, low clouds,

and marijuana.

In the glossy contemplation of the universe,

and what exactly it means

to be alive.

Today

Today is but one in the infinite number
that I have spent preparing to miss you;
just another in the unending string of days
where I look at every wall
and watch my grinning skull pound it to rubble.

I feel your fading, a growing emptiness,
a hunger for tragedy.

I count the days so I know how long I wished for an end.
How long I've hated myself for wishing.

I long to feel clean,
for water to scorch my tears to steam,
the vapor carries my hopes into the ether——
I aim them for your heart.
"May you find peace."

I lay on the filthy shower floor,
let the water soak into my skin,
watch my veins rise to the surface like dead fish,
close enough to cut.

We all die in a fraction of a minute—
life is comprised of fractions.
We are all half of a whole
until we find the other pieces
that complete us.

You have lost every other half you had—
even me.
And now I'm losing you in pieces.
You are in pieces.

                              I am torn

                                        to pieces.

To-Do List
What is a Waste of Time?

Find something worth spending time doing,

      like gazing at the heavens,

            or writing a song.

Find someone worth spending time with,

      even if they're not human.

            even if it's only myself.

Find the beauty in every day,

      even if it's only the sun rising,

            even if it's only myself.

There are a million things that I

      would like to do before I die,

            but do I really have the time?

Playing Like A Child in 2020

Yesterday I played
in the park like a child
I played and said,
"There's my cardio"
and the child said,
"There's your cardio."
And my friend said,
she plays or used to play
But she's wearing a dress
And the child says, "Mommy doesn't
want to show anything off."
The child says, "Mommy can't
eat pizza."
The child scoots on her scooter
in circles, one foot dangling,
occasionally finding ground or
the brake when she's only trying
to find her balance.
The child says,
"It's too crowded
over there."
But we play
where we are
like children

The Weight of Heartbreak

There are bones within my skin,
though you have not broken them,
I am now acutely aware of their weight.

I feel the way my arms rest
against my sides, or swish
as I walk, shoulders slumped, away.

My heart is more than heavy—
it does not swish as I walk,
but sinks further away from the sunlight

as if submerged by leagues
of murky water, decaying,
feeding other lifeforms with its rot.

What a weight this is,
pulling every inch of me down.

Perhaps I should cut my hair.

Remembering Mother

My mother was beautiful. She was tall with long red hair and a laugh that was full of music. She used to swing me in circles through the air, holding tight to my tiny hands that now look so much like hers. When she was home, we danced and sang together. My brothers and I were happy in the company of the one who made us, the piece that connected us. When she left, the sky seemed darker until she came home again. Those clouds were heralded by her thunderous temper. She would storm through the house, burdened by the anchor of home that kept her from the freedom of her life elsewhere. Or she would sit quietly crying, head bowed in prayer, pleading for strength until the desire overtook her and forced her away.

My mother was an addict. This fact was explained to us as gently as possible, as we were young children—my twin brother and I in kindergarten, and my older brother, not much farther into matriculation. "She's sick and can't stay here," my grandmother would say. I felt so bad for my mother when she cried for strength and prayed to God for salvation from the evil within her. I did not know then just how desperately she needed His mercy, and how desolate He had left her in its absence.

Every visit with my mother ended the same way; my grandmother would beg her to stay, but whatever power was granted to my mother by the Almighty was rendered useless by some obscure offense. She would leave again, bolting with an argument that really meant nothing. She could not be made to stay. Her mind was already pursuing other, darker gratifications. In my childish heart, I felt personally responsible for her leaving. I was not enough for her. I couldn't make her feel better. She sought solace somewhere else, and I believed it was my fault. I cried for her every time she left, sobbing in place of the words I wished I could say, "Please stay." I missed her violently, like a nightmare–long past and obscured by time and daylight. I remember with clarity, however, the last goodbye.

I watched her waving from the road, sun streaking copper through her thick, brick-red hair. I had already been sobbing, and her image was obstructed by the hot fog of my breath on the sliding glass doors. Her pale hand caressed the air in a farewell. I wished it was my hair her fingers gracefully brushed, and not the door of the yellow taxi come to take her from me. She packed lightly, as she always did. She never stayed long enough. My grandmother stood behind me, busying herself in the kitchen to keep from crying right along with me. Neither of us knew, but this would be the last time we say goodbye. The sun knew. It had already begun the work of erasing her image from my eyes, the brightness burning itself into my retinas, replacing her beautiful face with a blinding glare. She was nearly lost to me already. I felt the distance growing, even though I reached for her. My hand rested helplessly on the cold glass. She cast another look over her shoulder and lowered herself into the taxi, shut the door, and sped away. My grandmother placed her hand on my shoulder. I let mine fall to my side, its ghost captured in the cloud of my breath on the door. I was led away from the kitchen since there was nothing else to see. The distance grew ever farther between myself and my mother.

I did not know I would never see my mother alive again when she left that day, and perhaps it is only with the wisdom and heartbreak of retrospection, but I believe I felt the loneliness of her permanent absence long before the actual taking of her life. Perhaps that is why I cried for her so desperately that day, staring after her taxi even after it had borne her away from me across the two rivers and the hundred miles that separated us. I waited for her as I always did, every day or two asking when my mother would come home. I received the same answer as I always did. "Sometime soon, sweetie," my grandmother would say. I know now that she never knew when the wind would blow her only daughter back to her. She could only ever guess. I'm sure she never expected her daughter's fate, how the wind tore her to pieces before it carried her home.

On July 28th, 2004, my twin brother and I were on the school bus headed toward home. I remember the sun shining brightly against the backdrop of blue sky. I looked out the window as the bus wound its way through the hollers to my house. We lived on a mountain near the top. The houses sprawled along the hillside and down into the valley, encircled by the Guyandotte River and still more mountains. It was a beautiful, if dirty cage, keeping the poor segregated from the rest of the almost-as-poor city of Logan. The defeated houses rolled by slowly as we climbed, forgotten treasures littered every yard, decaying under the influence of the elements. Our yard was clean. Our house was beautiful, big, it looked like it held a family. My brother and I trotted unsuspectingly into the yard. We descended the few concrete steps into the grass and walked past our swing set and our little kitty whose name was Kitty. We had a concrete patio, scarcely furnished, and as we approached this, we noticed something was wrong. Most of my family—my grandmother and her sisters, my uncles, everyone sat or stood in our kitchen. I don't remember what the kitchen looked like anymore, but I remember them all standing there, staring at the television. My grandmother held her face in her hands, tears streaming from her eyes, as blue as the sky outside. We slid open the door. My grandmother gasped at us, sobbed loudly and cried for help from her sister, "Terri, please, I can't." We were ushered back out the door. My brother was already crying, though he couldn't have known yet. I was stunned and confused, silently waiting to find out what had broken my grandmother's heart.

"Kids," my aunt said gently, voice wavering from tears, "I'm sorry to have to tell you this." She broke here, could barely speak, "Your mommy got killed today. I'm so sorry." My brother could not contain himself. I do not know how he understood more than I the gravity of those words, but he did, for I only stood staring. I examined every block of the retaining wall that kept the mountainside from sliding, holding back the tons of rock and dirt waiting to bury us all. My aunt and my brother embraced each other, crying on each other's shoulders, my aunt apologizing and praying between gasps. I don't remember what I thought; the only thing I could do is stare and contemplate what it meant to be gone.

My mother lived in Huntington, West Virginia. She compromised her body, sanity, and family to accommodate her demons. She helped an old man, Charlie, with his daily activities, and when she died, he sent my brother and me golf sets. He "paid" for a week's vacation, but we had to leave after two nights because he, in fact, did not pay for a week's vacation. My grandmother called him a dirty old man. Matt Lauer called my mother a prostitute on the news. I knew what that meant, apparently, because I remember feeling indignant and angry at him for years. My grandmother called him a liar and told us it wasn't true, but I didn't care what anyone called her—I frequently drew my mother as an angel over my head. I sang all her favorite songs. I tried to summon her ghost through her remnant objects. I believed I succeeded, foolishly mistaking the shaking hands of a heartbroken child for an ethereal wind, disturbing one of her pearl necklaces that I dangled in front of me. "Please," I would beg, "if you're here, let me know." I worshipped her like a goddess. I prayed to her every night.

One day, I asked my grandmother when she thought my mother would be coming home, even though I knew she never would. My grandmother was quiet in her response, saying, "Honey, she won't be. But we'll see her again in Heaven." I think I only asked because I had already started to forget her. I thought the pain would bring her back. I thought getting over her was disrespectful, so I tried to live in the pain. I convinced myself that she was alive, even though I had seen her at the funeral. I saw red-haired strangers and knew it was her, living a secret life free from the burden of drugs or family. Romantic, like the poetry and stories she left behind in notebooks. My grandmother used to beg me to finish them, but I don't believe in those kinds of happy endings anymore.

As I grew older, I grew angry. I thought my mother was weak for choosing her vices over her family. I thought I was unworthy of love. In high school, I began to obsess over answers. I read through all those old notebooks. I read articles online, her obituary, and the poem given out at her funeral. She was consumed by her demons, but she never forgave herself or forgot her family. It took a long time to forgive my grandmother for lying to me about my mother's life; I thought by not knowing the truth, I didn't know *her*. Her loss left a hole in my heart that I filled first with hurt, then anger, and eventually understanding more about the evils of addiction, about what addiction can do to a person. My mother exists in my mind as a complex enigma, battling her own mind, trying to reconcile her desire for freedom and love, for drugs, for her family, with the reality of the life she led. Would she have predicted her eventual demise? I'm not sure if there is a God. But, I know if there is, He listened to her desperate prayers as she clung to the lifeboat of her family, even if her own flailing is what sunk it. He knows she always tried.

From the Distance of Space

I am drawn to those parts of the ocean that,
when pictured from the distance of space,
extend on and on into blackness.
The depths remind me that I am small,
that there is a tiny sun at my feet and I
am in revolution around it.

I am drawn to those parts of land,
that when pictured from the distance of space,
ascend from the deep to become mountains.
Mountains are self-destructive,
but they float, too.

I would like to swim under the Earth—
       kiss the tiny sun at my feet.
Why can't I afford to eat?
Why does it even matter?
You cannot see an empty stomach
from the distance of space.

Curtains

The sun has set on the year, and the evening hours before this darkness did not blaze away in golden splendor. The sun fought for this respite, this transition to the other side. There were clouds, blustery winds, and storms so terrible that the life-giving glory and promise of warmth were buried. Those gazing toward the empty, gray heavens wondered, shivering, whether there was even a sun left to set or rise at all.

But set, it did. Now comes the disorienting, otherworldly hours of pre-dawn. Human language shies from the challenge of describing this purgatory. Is it morning? Only by the loosest definition of the word. Is it night? Well, it's dark, yes, but the sun is coming. Any moment, the sky will raise the velvet curtain of night to reveal the brightening stage of day—lights up, places, the show is about to start.

I am the sole actor on this stage. But I don't have the lines for this scene because I don't have the words to say, now. You were the director, you set the stage, and I have been left to carry this play on my own.

And the show must go on, even if you are not here to watch it.

I feel as though I missed my cue. I feel as though I tried to nap through a storm and slept through the dawn. I have woken to that undefined space of time between night and the light of morning. I'm staring, cold, waiting for the sun to rise. This year, this set, this show, this new day has dawned and you are not here and I have not learned those lines. I have not rehearsed this. The blocking isn't natural when you aren't on stage with me.

And to think I used to feel relief when you weren't in the crowd to watch me. Your gaze felt too heavy then—your heart swelled too much with pride and I did not think I had enough within me to fill it. I wonder if anyone would have.

The dark of this brand-new day is as big, I think, as that space left unfilled in your heart. The fear that I will be consumed by it is paralyzing. I feel so lost without the warm light of the sun.

But people are not responsible for the sky. I cannot bring the morning. I am only here to watch the sun rise or set, or count the stars. I am here to stand in this purgatory and watch the hues of the sky lighten by the minute.

Any moment now...

Jigsaw Pieces

There is not enough

        Magic in the language of

                Humans to

express the

        Freedom of the mind.

There is no

        Liberation comparable to that of

                Being one with not only

yourself,

        but with Everything.

All life exists as a

        Jigsaw puzzle—

Individual pieces making

        a Beautiful picture, impossibly

fitting together like the fibers of a fine piece of

        Silk.

What's wrong with being an end piece?

        Nothing.

What's wrong with being a middle piece?

                           Nothing.

Every other piece would mean

                           Nothing

if another was missing; just an

                  Unintelligible

                          gathering of

                Pieces.

When the puzzle is finished,

               you will realize not a single piece is

               Jumbled.

Every one had a

        Place.

About the Author

Alexis Cremeans was born in rural Logan, West Virginia, and raised by her grandmother. Though circumstances were at times difficult, Alexis learned perseverance and strength through her grandmother and aunts and found company in her siblings.

Growing up, she always sought to express herself through writing in an effort to better understand herself and the world around her. She followed her passion through college, earning a Literary Studies and Creative Writing degree from Marshall University.

Alexis now resides in southern Ohio with her loving husband and beautiful two-year-old daughter.

Blending transcendental, environmental, and cosmic influences, Alexis uses poetry to explore difficult, beautiful, natural, and mysterious parts of life. She wrestles with death, heartbreak, love, and loneliness within the pages of her debut poetry collection, Orphan Poetry.

READ INDIE. STAY AWESOME.
MORE BOOKS FROM THE HENLO PRESS

Glass Mountain by Laura Treacy Bentley

The Dictionary Game by Mike Hornyak

These Old Familiar Rooms by Mike Hornyak

Extreme Human Overload by Diana Johnson

The Mother of Monsters by M.A. Elliott

A Ghost of Spring by A.B. Hooser

The Wonderfully Wild Adventures of Kana and Charlie: Monstrous Mo and the Stolen Apples by Josh Taylor, Illustrated by Jeremiah Morgan

304 Monsters by Stephen Bias

West By God by Tyler Bell

Deadly Choices: Will You Survive? | Camp Meltaway by Tiffany and Caitlyn Pace

Old Bones:Volume One by Various

A Shade of Winter by A.B. Hooser

Mumblings: West Virginia Horror Stories by Caitlyn Pace

Afterwords by Stephen Bias

www.ingramcontent.com/pod-product-compliance
Lightning Source LLC
Chambersburg PA
CBHW030527130626
46549CB00007B/3127